Squawk!

Social

Media

for the

Solitary

Bird

Dedication

Dedicated to Dave the Knave (and Polly the Parrot).
Your humor and courage inspire me.

Parrot photo on cover by Psyberartist
https://www.flickr.com/photos/psyberartist/7767885876/
https://www.flickr.com/people/psyberartist/
Creative Commons Attribution 2.0 Generic license

This book and other products to aid creative development may be ordered directly from the publisher at:

www.parallelmindzz.com
tools & toys for creative people

Library of Congress Cataloging-in-Publication Data

Marr, Aliyah

Squawk! Social media for the solitary bird—find your flock, express yourself, and stand out from the crowd / Aliyah Marr—1st ed

Copyright © 2014 Aliyah Marr. All rights reserved.

ISBN-13: 978-1503327566
ISBN-10: 1503327566

1. Social Media—Twitter, Linked In. 2. Marketing—Social Media.
3. Branding. 4. Success in Business. 5. Internet Marketing.

think
ǝpᴉsuᴉ
down ™

Contents

"Squawk?"

Squawk! is a collection of ideas—or seeds—about how to use social media for professional purposes. It shows how to promote without advertising and how to market without marketing: how to gather a flock of people with similar interests, and communicate with them effectively.

A new look at the contemporary phenomenon of social media, *Squawk!* contains common sense suggestions on how to work with an amazing grass-roots revolutionary movement.

This book is dedicated to the art of professional networking and personal branding; it shows you how to represent yourself, your cause, or your business in social media. *Squawk!* sets out to show how our society has changed with the tools of social media, and how you can easily participate in this social media revolution.

—introduction—

A Bird's Eye View

How can you professionally represent yourself, communicate your cause, and brand your business in social media without sacrificing your entire life to do it?

Squawk! is ideal for the small business or consultant who has little or no advertising budget, or who realizes that advertising doesn't work in today's world.

This book is for you if you want to:

- Create an honest no-hype presence on the web for yourself or for your business

- Gain a real following of people that are listening

- Establish whom you are without self-promoting or advertising

- Establish yourself as an authority in your field

- Supply real information that helps potential customers to make informed decisions

- Build an image of who you are and what you do in your reader's minds

- Become more effective in how you communicate

- Stand out in the social media forest, not be lost in the meaningless trees of content

-:-:-:-:-

Most books on social media are little more than sales hype. They do not take into account that the grass-roots movement of social media resists all normal advertising and sales techniques. Think of the last time you were grateful for an ad on Facebook or for a screaming email blast in your mailbox, and you will realize what I mean.

Social media is not sales and it is not e-commerce, but it is an effective communication and branding tool that can establish you as an authority in your field, and support your services or product line with real information and content.

Social media changes nearly daily; it is an impossible task to keep up with all the platforms that are available to the modern user. If you try to have a presence on each platform, the sheer volume of work will keep you from running your business or living your life.

Social media can be a trap for those trying to achieve huge amounts of friends or fans; it is hole that you drop your precious time down, unless you know what you are doing. This book is not a how-to for each form of social media, instead it encourages you to "see the big picture" of who you are and what you do, and communicate this no matter where you are, from online in Facebook to offline in an elevator.

Squawk! encourages you to be real—online and off—to represent yourself in a way that communicates sincerity and professionalism online. This book outlines real marketing techniques that help you create an image of who you are and what you do in the mind of the user. You can use the tools of branding to establish yourself as the expert in your field, your products or your services and what benefits they will bring the buyer, or your business and how responsive it is to its users.

Social media is the support system, the communication system, and as such can be the life-blood of a modern business. It is a powerful adjunct to any brand or organization. It can help you gain clients and retain current clients.

A new look at the contemporary phenomenon of social media, *Squawk!* contains common sense suggestions on how to work with all forms of social media. For the everyman or everywoman who wants to exercise his/her voice in professional social media, this book is a quirky, unconventional approach, a motley collection of ideas—or seeds—about how to use social media for professional purposes.

This book shows how to be effective and honest on social media; how to promote without advertising, and how to market without marketing: how to gather a flock of fans, and communicate with them effectively. If you need a how-to on the specifics of any one social media platform or shining, inspirational stories of financial success, I recommend buying a different book.

New technology should not make us into a technician or slave to the application, but instead, it should free the individual to live a better life. The purpose of this book is to help you better use the tool of social media to achieve this same goal.

-:-:-:-

Squawk! is a Think Upside-Down book. A think upside-down* idea is a counter-culture, creative, and fresh way to look at a given topic. It turns the topic upside-down and looks at the underside; it sees the forest for the trees; it gets right to the heart of the matter; it frees you to stand out from the crowd.

The funny thing is that a think upside-down concept is obvious, but like the proverbial elephant in the living room, it is often too big to see. That is why I have decided that the anagram T.H.U.N.K. is appropriate for the idea that is so obvious but unseen. THUNK is the sound that something really big makes when it hits the ground: it is also the sound that a new, blatantly obvious idea makes when it hits my head.

A THUNK upside your head
There is an even bigger change afoot that hardly anyone ever sees: our tools have a tendency to change us at such a fundamental level that we can't even see what is happening.

Think about how your life has changed since the advent of cell phones, texting, and the Internet. We all know that modern communications have changed our lives by giving us ease, convenience, and speed, but how many of us can see how this technology has changed the way we think?

Before we decide to adapt, use, or discard these changes in our lives we should understand what they mean to us personally, and to us culturally. Only a new upside-down look at our old world view can allow us to see everything clearly, so we can decide what we should do, individually and collectively.

* I coined the term "think upside-down" in my first book, *Parallel Mind, The Art of Creativity.*

Chicken Hawks Beware!

Some people are willing to swallow any promise that might make them easy money. The latest target is social media. It seems that everyone these days wants to know how to get social media to pay.

Marketing mavens struggle to advertise on social media; content mills try to find a way to squeeze the maximum amount of keywords in 140 characters or less; bloggers want to clock enough traffic to qualify for high-paying ads. Linked In serves up one-line ads that guarantee you a lucrative social media manager job at the end of an expensive online course.

This book is not intended to be a primer for corporate entities, marketing mavens, SEO keyword content mill workers, hysterical bean-counting "give us your last bean!" advertising professionals, networking pundits, get-rich-quick quacks, or self-acclaimed experts of any kind.

If you are looking for the quick fix, if you see social media as the perfect income-from-home-job, or if you are a marketer looking for a cheap replacement for ads, this book is probably not for you. This is not a book of guaranteed moneymaking techniques or platform-specific information.

Squawk! aspires to show how social media has engendered social change. This change is a fundamental shift away from "business as usual" in many fields, such as marketing, advertising, information technology, media, publishing, internet, and businesses of all kinds.

Without an understanding of the "big picture" of these changes, an average user might be inclined to try to make social media adapt to old, outdated ideas and techniques. But if you know what is really happening, you can better navigate this amazing medium, and use it in a way that enhances your life while becoming an effective participant in one of the most significant grassroots revolution of the century.

Chapter 1

—advertising is dead—

Scratching in the Dirt for Worms

The old world of advertising attempts to trick people into buying; broadcast media supports advertising with content that is meant to make sales for the sponsors. The news is just a means to make sure people stay glued to the screen so they can see the advertising messages.

The people on social media naturally move away from the brainwashing of advertising and thus are part of a revolution: a revolution that reinstates community at the head of the state instead of political figures.

With the emphasis shifted to community and what the community wants, the end of what I like to call "trickster advertising" looms very near, and the advertisers—on the web or otherwise—are running scared. On the web, this amounts to trying to find more keywords like chickens scratching in the dirt for worms.

E-commerce marketing mavens rely upon complex schemes to put out content embedded with keywords that match what people search for on the web. Trying to make content based upon keywords results in an incomprehensible miss-mash for the reader and eventual discrediting of the content deliverer.

Social media gives people two things: a means to express themselves, and a way in which to form new smaller social units, to gather together in virtual communities. In essence, it is giving people a way to have a virtual social revolution; this will eventually erase political boundaries, and create new nations founded upon likeness of mind rather than on geographical location.

The freedom of having a voice on a global platform is a heady experience. Once freedom is obtained, people will fight to retain it. If a social media platform tries to become an advertising platform, people will eventually dump it for something newer and more fun and expressive.

The genie of personal expression cannot be easily stuffed back into the shampoo bottle; the one from the advertising era that tells us to "rinse and repeat" to increase more shampoo sales while irreparably damaging our hair.

Chickens With a Rather Sordid History

The beginning of social media marketing can be traced to email lists. In the early days of Internet marketing these were formed from non-voluntary, or pseudo-voluntary lists of individuals. Many of the people on these stone-age mailing lists didn't even know they were on them. Marketing was up to its old trick of broadcasting to the faceless masses, trying to blast them through their email boxes instead of through their televisions.

As early Internet users started to experience a deluge of spam in their mailboxes, and the servers were swamped by mail going to thousands of recipients, promoters were forced by the beleaguered geeks and aggravated populace to adopt what Seth Godin coined as Permission Marketing. The misuse of email advertising campaigns resulted in the birth of the double opt-in: promoters with a message to deliver have to entice the user to join their list, and then ask for his confirmation.

The Chicken and the Egg

Advertisers and sales people intent on gathering more fans and friends seem to think that people will automatically bond with them like new chicks straight out of the egg if they continue to blast out new messages to the public.

But social media works on the naturally occurring principle of social gathering: the "birds of a feather flock together" rule. People on the broad plain of the Internet are looking for a smaller clustering to form a social group; they are looking for people who think like them.

The need to form a social group comes from a need to offset the virtually infinite vastness of the Internet, and it is a direct reaction to the advertisers' need to profit from it. So, there is a push and pull in social media, from those who wish to retain the grassroots and intimate nature of a social gathering, and from those on the other hand who wish to turn it into another form of e-commerce.

The more that e-commerce businesses try to profit from the people in social media, the more the people of social media will resist it. Social media has turned into a revolutionary movement, affecting everything from schooling to politics.

A Bunch of Dumb Clucks

In the now waning era of consumerism, the individual was seen as a dumb consumer: his brain, a blank screen waiting for multiple ad impressions. Advertisers could feed a consumer a bunch of TV ads, make him compete with the Joneses for their products, and deliver planned obsolescence instead of a quality product.

Broadcast advertising over the medium of TV was the lifeblood of the recently deceased consumer era. The advertisers and corporations redefined people as buying units with disposable cash. TV became the medium of choice for dishing out the propaganda in the form of ads. Individuals were labeled as consumers; this was the defining moment in the advertising era.

Chapter 2
—the social media revolution—

A Democracy in the Hen House

Fast-forward a few years to the start of viral marketing: I am not sure if corporations and marketers get this yet, but viral communication works both ways. After all, if you can market a product using the viral opinions of the consumer, that same consumer has the power to completely bash your product, company, or idea as well.

The Democratization of Media

The emergence of popular outlets for social expression such as YouTube, FaceBook, and Twitter has changed online media in an unanticipated way. When anyone can contribute or edit the vast encyclopedia of human knowledge, what happens to society?

The average person has learned not to trust what he hears in traditional media.

What can you trust, and whom can you trust? The emergence of social networking and viral marketing in this same era is provides a clue to what may be happening. Corporations would love to control this amazing medium as a way to advertise their products to the consumer, but it can backfire. Social media is very sensitive to hype and is quick to expose inconsistencies and flaws. It would be just as easy to get negative as well as positive results using viral marketing and social networking.

The positive result of this movement is that it may allow a real accountability to emerge in the economic as well as the political arena. It has the potential to finally hold leaders responsible,; to make companies accountable to their consumers and the environmental impact of production.

With great power comes great responsibility.

The power of free speech is in the hands of the many instead of the few as media has resulted in the democratization of the media. Commercial and political interests will strive to control and utilize this power to their own ends.

Viral marketing is a hot topic among marketers. They ask themselves the conversations on social media can be used for profit and how they can control what is being said. Bloggers are romanced by corporate entities and some are even paid to write corporate messages and product review as if they are sources of information that are independent of their employers.

As the uncle of Spiderman said, "With great power comes great responsibility." Democracy in whatever form has the annoying tendency to mutate into something else, while pretending to have remained true to form.

Perhaps the book "Animal Farm" was not really about communism at all, but about how information gets mutated by those in authority. Information can only be trusted if it remains independent of commercial or political interests, as the debacle of commercial media in present times has proved.

A Revolution of Birds

Squawk! announces that a revolution has taken place under our very noses. The new medium of social media has created a new grassroots movement. It is such a big change that almost no one notices what happened. Social media shows us that a new paradigm has evolved. You can see it in the verbiage:

Old paradigm verbiage
Consumers, corporate power, mass marketing, advertising, planned obsolescence, email blasts, broadcasting.

New paradigm verbiage
Individualists, informed buyers reporting on products and corporations, freedom of choice, democratized media, viral messaging, conversation, democratic media, inclusion & participation, flocking behavior, community, global reach.

Or to put it more succinctly, the old paradigm of the advertising age and consumerism is being replaced by a new era of individualism, free choice, and democratic grass-roots viral media.

Love Birds

The concept of consumerism is based upon an idea of mass movement, and led us away from the ideals of individuality and freedom. People—consumers—were expected to be dumb clucks that needed repetitive ad messages to brainwash them to pick up quantities of bath tissue and tooth-rotting cola next time they were down at the store.

"I trust people like me"

The grassroots phenomenon of social media had a precedent: cable TV. Cable started out as an alternative to broadcast TV. Its appeal was two-fold: it was locally produced and it was advertising-free. Local production put the power back into the hands of the people; they were more likely to know the people they saw on screen—being local meant they could identify with them as "people like me."

In the Edelman Trust Barometer report in 2008, the majority (58%) of the respondents reported they most trusted company or product information coming from "people like me" inferred to be information from someone they trusted. People today are drawn to trust—and eventually buy—from those that are familiar to them: those they have chosen to be in their flock.

Cable TV died as a social medium when advertising crept in. The individuals that have come to love social media are not about to allow their voice to be drowned out by advertising on social media. Ultimately this battle is changing society at a root level. We are quickly moving from a description of the individual as a brainless consumer to that of an expressive, empowered, and vocal individual.

Chapter 3
—defining social media—

The Twittering Machine

For a definition of social media I went to the big mama of all social media, my writing companion, my trusty unpaid editor: Wikipedia:

The term social media refers to the use of web-based and mobile technologies to turn communication into interactive dialogue. Social media are media for social interaction, as a superset beyond social communication, but mainly still communicating just interactively using ubiquitously accessible and scalable communication techniques.

Social media can take on many different forms, including Internet forums, weblogs, social blogs, microblogging, wikis, podcasts, photographs or pictures, video, rating and social bookmarking.

By applying a set of theories in the field of media research (social presence, media richness) and social processes (self-presentation, self-disclosure) Kaplan and Haenlein created a classification scheme for different social media types in their Business Horizons article published in 2010.

According to Kaplan and Haenlein there are six different types of social media: collaborative projects (e.g. Wikipedia), blogs and microblogs (e.g. Twitter), content communities (e.g. YouTube), social networking sites (e.g. Facebook), virtual game worlds (e.g. World of Warcraft), and virtual social worlds (e.g. Second Life).

Technologies include: blogs, picture-sharing, vlogs, wall-postings, email, instant messaging, music-sharing, crowdsourcing, and voice over IP, to name a few. Many of these social media services can be integrated via social network aggregation platforms.

The View Outside the Chicken Coop

Here is how the analysts see social media.

The Honeycomb Structure of Social Media

In a 2011 article, Jan H. Kietzmann, Kristopher Hermkens, Ian P. McCarthy and Bruno S. Silvestre state that the seven building blocks that define social media are identity, conversations, sharing, presence, relationships, reputation, and groups.

The Seven Building Blocks of Social Media

1. Identity

This block represents the extent to which users reveal their identities in a social media setting. This can include disclosing information such as name, age, gender, profession, location, and also information that portrays users in certain ways.

2. Conversations

This block represents the extent to which users communicate with other users in a social media setting. Many social media sites are designed primarily to facilitate conversations among individuals and groups. These conversations happen for all sorts of reasons. People tweet, blog, etcetera to meet new like-minded people, to find true love, to build their self-esteem, or to be on the cutting edge of new ideas or trending topics. Yet others see social media as a way of making their message heard and positively impacting humanitarian causes, environmental problems, economic issues, or political debates.

3. Sharing
This block represents the extent to which users exchange, distribute, and receive content. The term 'social' often implies that exchanges between people are crucial. In many cases, however, sociality is about the objects that mediate these ties between people—the reasons why they meet online and associate with each other.

4. Presence
This block represents the extent to which users can know if other users are accessible. It includes knowing where others are, in the virtual world and/or in the real world, and whether they are available.

5. Relationships
This block represents the extent to which users can be related to other users. Two or more users have some form of association that leads them to converse, share

objects of sociality, meet up, or simply just list each other as a friend or fan.

6. Reputation
This block represents the extent to which users can identify the standing of others, including themselves, in a social media setting. Reputation can have different meanings on social media platforms.

In most cases, reputation is a matter of trust, but since information technologies are not yet good at determining such highly qualitative criteria, social media sites rely on 'mechanical Turks': tools that automatically aggregate user-generated information to determine trustworthiness.

7. Groups
This block represents the extent to which users can form communities and sub communities. The more 'social' a network becomes, the bigger the group of friends, followers, and contacts.

Bird's Eye View

Q. What is social media?

A. It is a grass-roots movement, a running conversation between individuals of like interests; an interactive, multimedia forum of democratic voices, a community of empowered individuals. Social media is what media was supposed to be: it is the voice of the everyman/woman; an essential partner in any society that aspires to the values of democratic action, individual expression, and free speech. Social media is an ever-shifting collection of voices, special interests, groups of associated individuals; who may or may not admit to being a member of any community.

Q. What is social media NOT?

A. It is not advertising, not broadcasting, not a platform for self-aggrandizement.

Q. Who is the social media individual?

A. He/she is a pioneer of conversation and a resident of a global community, a willing, conscious participant of viral concepts and ideas; he/she values free speech over propaganda, and values the independent expression of his/her neighbor over official versions.

Bird Seeds

The phenomenon of social media has changed us in some very fundamental ways.

The empowered individual powers social media

The base unit of the social media phenomenon is the individual. Now the individual has all the power in his hands: he has choice on what he sees and which global community he belongs to.

No longer fed ads while waiting for the content, no longer part of the faceless mass of brainless consumers, the empowered individual can affect which companies survive, and which die; he can vote with his attention and with his words as well as with his wallet.

A society of lateral leaders

A community of individuals cannot exist under the old, outdated rules of autocratic corporate structure. Instead of a community of followers gathered around a single leader or team of leaders, social media is decentralized and democratic.

This has resulted in the emergence of a new kind of individual: the lateral leader. A lateral leader—a term that I coined a few years ago—is an individual who leads only when other individuals respond to what they have to say at any given moment. They maintain their authority only over their chosen subject matter, or area of expertise, not over their peers. A lateral leader is respected by her peers for her knowledge and contribution to her community.

Quality over quantity
Counter to popular opinion, it is quality not quantity that counts in the world of professional social media. You want quality conversations, relationships, links, communities, and contacts online, and off.

Community-building
A community is formed from a group of individuals. In social media, the individual volunteers to be part of your group, or asks others to be part of a group he has formed.

A grassroots movement
Social media is essentially a leaderless community; it resembles a democracy. People who use social media tend to resist following leaders (see "Individuals" above), but don't mind following other individuals.

Historically, this is true of all grassroots movements. Their members are diverse and spread out. Like the roots of grass, they are difficult to eradicate because there is no one central root. This is what makes a grassroots movement so powerful; the individual voice counts, and is equal to all other voices.

The new global village

In the oh-so-distant past of the broadcasting era, you didn't feel like you were part of a global community. You were separated from your distant brother by your inability to communicate with him. Information in the broadcast era was one-way. Television supported the official version of reality, and reinforced established personal and societal limitations and beliefs.

Even the early Internet era was restricted by the lack of a structure that would have facilitated meeting and conversing with others. Now, social media allows us to easily meet people in every country. The only potential barriers now are language and the availability of computers and Internet service.

Recognition

In a leaderless society the individual shines. Like the Wild West of yore, it's a bit of a free-for-all. Social media gunslingers vie for the pithiest repartee, the best content and links. The person with the best conversation and relationships is rewarded by growing popularity and renown (see below).

Conversation

When you have a party, conversation between the individuals naturally ensues. The kind of conversation at the party is determined by the kind of individuals at the party. Social media is a conversation between individuals and between groups of individuals.

You Can Tweet Too

What software or applications qualify as social media?

- Blogs (Wordpress)

- Micro Blogs (Twitter)

- Personal Networks (Facebook)

- Professional Networks (Linked In)

- Collaborative Projects (Wikipedia)

- Content Communities (YouTube)

- Grassroots Media (Blog Talk radio)

- Distribution engines (Blip.tv, Hoot Suite)

This is by no means a complete list; new kinds of social media crop up every day. What is important is not to understand how to use every platform, but to understand how to use social media in general, and thus how you want to participate.

consumers

OLD THINKING	SHORT-TERM GAINS
a mass of uneducated consumers	MARKET
the consumer is a stupid buying machine who will buy anything if we appeal to his greed and ego	THE INDIVIDUAL
advertising + marketing + large amounts of money = sales	SALES
broadcast your ideas to the masses	COMMUNICATION
official sources	MEDIA
the media, corporations, and government to protect your interests	TRUST
advertising	CONTENT
get as many followers as possible	GOAL
responsibility stops after the sale	FOLLOW-UP
the one with the most fans wins	GAME WINNER
paper bank notes that are no longer backed by gold	CURRENCY

community

LONG-TERM GOALS	NEW THUNK
MARKET	communities of smart individuals
THE INDIVIDUAL	the individual is smart, and does his research before buying
SALES	branding + information + customer service = loyal customers
COMMUNICATION	conversations between equals
MEDIA	user-generated media
TRUST	people that you know personally
CONTENT	information on demand
GOAL	make & sustain relationships
FOLLOW-UP	customer service is part of the sale
GAME WINNER	the more qualified people you know, the more successful you are
CURRENCY	your creativity, integrity, contacts, relationships, skills, & reputation

Chapter 4
—how to use social media—

ADVERTISING AGE vs. SOCIAL MEDIA ERA

Consumers vs. Informed Buyers
Advertising vs. Information
Broadcasting vs. Conversations
Official vs. User-Generated Content
Customers vs. Neighbors
Markets vs. Communities

Summed up in a Quick Tweet

Social Media has moved us:

- From a what to a who

- From centralized to decentralized

- From advertisements to information

- From consumers to communities

- From traditional media to user-generated media

- From mass media marketing to viral marketing

- From voice-mail to customer service

- From broadcast advertising to conversations

Practice Your Song

Social media is about personality
Social media is about your style of communicating; your way of relating. Personality and style are everything on a medium that emphasizes the power of the individual. If you are a geek with a fear of social interaction of any kind, or if you never wanted to share your toys as a child, you might want to consider another career or medium.

Social media is interactive
Social media is not broadcasting, it is not advertising, and it is not a linear storyline: social media is interaction between equals (see allergens below).

Social media is brief
Keep everything as short as possible. Use the KISS philosophy: Keep It Simple Stupid. I prefer to say, Keep It Super Simple.

ANNOUNCEMENT: think Tweet, instead of infomercial.

BRANDING: think 10-second station ID instead of shopping network program.

PRODUCT: think hyperlink to more information instead of long explanations.

TUTORIAL: think bullet points or short movie instead of technical manual.

ADVERTISEMENT: don't think "ad" at all; give benefits, and allow the user to decide.

CUSTOMER SERVICE: think human instead of voice mail automaton.

Social media is inclusive and participatory by nature. Relationship is about inclusion. Relationship is about interactive participation; there is a natural give and take in any healthy relationship.

Social Media Marketing: You Have to Give to Get
These days, content is king. In order to get the attention on online media that you desire, it seems that you have to provide lots of free content first.

If you wish to market yourself you have to prove your value to your market (community). It's like applying for a job. If you are looking for work, you have to present a resume that proves that you have the education, the experience and the skills to do the work.

Social media and the Webscape work the same way. Unless you have an established brand behind you, you will have to prove that you can provide value first, before you can even think of making a sale.

All great entrepreneurs have had to start the same way: they had to prove that their product was worth buying. In the past, they hired advertising firms to help them promote their products or service. Today, the field is leveled by the availability of free online social media platforms. Anyone can promote their services on the Internet; so several new hurdles have developed.

One hurdle remains from the past: an image of professionalism. Quality branding and professional design cannot be underestimated. One of the new hurdles that brands have to face is the idea of providing value. One can do that through providing useful content. This is why blogs and micro blogs are so important today. The ideal blog is updated often enough to be valued by both robots (search engines) and by loyal followers.

The trick is to give away valuable information without overburdening the viewer (such as the Twitterer who posts too often) or giving away the farm. I have noticed a huge range of Twitter habits; from once a week to once every half-hour. Someone like Guy Kawasaki seems to update constantly, something that I don't mind only because his updates are interesting to me.

As to the subject matter of the content itself; make sure that you hold to your declared subject, the narrower, the better. Unless you are a movie star with a huge following of loyal followers, avid for the latest tidbits about the intimate habits of your favorite poodle, it is preferable to have a smaller following of targeted members than a huge following of people who can't remember why they started following you. These people are the same ones who will drop you like a bad date.

What is the final purpose of providing all this free information? That is for you to determine. You may want to get them on your newsletter, which you should also provide for free, in most cases.

Or you may want to make an immediate sale. You will have to determine how to best ask for that sale.

Perhaps you don't want to even do that, perhaps you allow ads on your blog or website, and that gives you revenue. Some people don't want to sell anything at all, and these people are simply attempting to establish their name and their brand. Many users on the Internet expect only free information, so this may be a marriage made in heaven.

Many people are concerned about giving away information, especially if their main product is information. This is a valid concern, but it takes a bit of finessing to be able to give away valuable information without giving away your product. I prefer to err on the side of generosity.

I give away a great deal of information because I know that the right client will be attracted to me by the quality of my work. A potential client who does not resonate with my words will drop my newsletter, and will never become a client. That is OK with me. I want only clients that appreciate what I can do for them, and will value my advice.

Use social media to display your knowledge
If you have specialized knowledge, social media is one way to get known for what you know. Start a blog, a Twitter account, post on YouTube, and run

an Internet radio show to establish your reputation. Start a Linked In account, so that your resume has a permanent place to reside, and so you have a place to cultivate important professional connections.

Step One to Building Your Reputation Online

If you want to be known professionally register on a professional networking site such as Linked In. Think of Linked In as your ever-present online resume. This free service allows you to build your profile, find connections from your address book, and make and receive recommendations. You can make contact with some people who you may not have been able to find otherwise. You can receive testimonials and recommendations from clients and associates.

Once you have entered some of your connections, then go back to your profile page to see happened to your information. When I did this, I saw that each of my connections have links to other people, which effectively extends your reach.

The person who has the most connections wins in the networking game; the more connections your connections have, the more opportunities can come your way.

The recommendations other people have submitted for me enhance my reputation online. Anyone who may want to employ me for my expertise will want to check my reputation before they hire me, and now all they have to do is check my Linked In account. There they can read my professional profile, see my photo, and read the recommendations from satisfied clients and associates that show me to be a professional who knows my field, has integrity, and gets the job done.

Social media is about relevance

Birds of a feather flock together and sing the same song. Be careful that you know who your flock is, and choose your words accordingly. Have you ever been at a party where someone started talking about a topic that didn't interest the group? Be careful to be relevant, especially if you are engaging in professional social media.

Let's say that you are an employer, and you are reviewing a potential employee's Linked In profile. You would want to see jobs that are relevant to your open position. You would want to see that the potential employee has expertise in their topic; you may have even found your candidate participating in or leading a group discussion. Your interest is peaked.

Social media is about agreement
With all this talk about individuality, it is still agreement that solidifies any group. By picking your topic and your flock carefully, you will seldom have to worry about agreeing with your fellows. And disagreement can then be a lively discussion or debate among friends.

Social media is about repetition
Repetition makes your point. On Twitter it lives as retweets, and it is a way of complimenting another, it is a way to get them to notice you, and even a way to get to know others better.

Social media is about service
Corporate or business interests can use social media as a way to provide excellent, timely customer service, or tech support. This medium adapts well to short streams of on-demand information. Longer explanations, or tutorial movies can be accessed from links.

If a corporate or business hires a social media service manager, they should make sure that the user can access the information they need when they need it.

Chapter 5

—how NOT to use social media—

Bird Allergens

The following practices and attitudes are guaranteed to make any otherwise healthy bird fall dead off its perch.

Social media is allergic to advertising

Today, TV ads are cheap because nearly hardly anyone markets their products that way anymore. The advent of cable TV gave the populace a taste of commercial-free entertainment, whose early promise has been eclipsed today by the ubiquitous shopping-channel; which has ironically replaced the traditional TV show with a single non-stop commercial, called the shopping channel.

The web gave us the mouse: a tool that allowed us the vote on what we would watch—if nothing else, we could opt out of inane splash screen animations made by Flash amateurs. Advertisers suddenly had to account for everything in their ads.

On TV the average ad takes 30 seconds out of our lives. The attention span of the user on the web went from something like 10 seconds in the early days of the web to a mere two or three seconds today. People are much more sophisticated in their tastes and are absolutely allergic to any kind of advertising.

What precipitated this allergy? As with any food allergy, it was caused by a diet consisting of too much advertising. The death of advertising was caused by the unending deluge of ads that the public was subjected to over the decades. As a result, the social media individual is very, very resistant to advertising.

Social media is allergic to follower mills
In the early days of social media, people thought that the goal of the game was to amass as many followers as possible. This resulted in follower mills—automatic or semi-automatic follower technology. With one of these tricky little ploys followers alighted on Twitter pages like a flock of starlings in a tree at nightfall. As any seasoned marketer knows, if your fans aren't part of your target market (your community) they are worth next to nothing.

Social media is allergic to stuffiness
The opposite of the warm-and-fuzzy, down-home feeling of a grassroots movement is the oxygen-poor stuffiness of the corporate boardroom. That doesn't mean that if you have a brand to represent, or a product to sell, you shouldn't go about your task

in a stuffy, corporate manner. Instead you want to generate a feeling of accessibility, friendliness, and if possible, an attitude of fun.

Think *Apple* instead of *IBM*, a game instead of an accounting ledger, or a conversation among peers instead of a corporate annual report. If your blog, Twitter account, and Linked In presence is easy to read, fun, and approachable, people will want to relate to you. Voluntary relationships are the key to social media.

Social media is allergic to broadcasting
Until the advent of interactive design—exemplified by games, websites, and kiosks—our world consisted of linear media. A linear piece, as opposed to a non-linear piece, allows the user very little control over his experience.

Think of a video: you have the following limited options: start, stop, pause, fast-forward, and reverse. The broadcast medium relies on the concept of a rigid timeline with a beginning, middle, and an end. This idea of linear time hasn't changed since the days of ancient Greek morality plays. Television carried forward the ancient concept of the teaching story. A story with an underlying message is funneled into the minds of the television audience. The concept of the teaching story was appropriated from other art forms to sell things to people watching shows on TV. The story might be the show, or it might be the 30-second commercial, but the user had little or no control over the delivery of the message or over the content of the message.

The Internet is an example of an interactive user experience. A website may have a message or a brand image to deliver, but the user gets to choose his path at any time, even if he just wants to opt out of the website entirely.

The advent of the two-way conversation that preceded social media started with comment boxes on blogs, and with texting on phones. This is a conversation between equals, which is the beginning of a relationship.

Because users have experienced the freedom of inter-active media for years now, they are impatient with corporate broadcasting and with one-way communi-cation. If you try to use social media to broadcast your message to your supposed audience, without allowing them to interact with you or converse, you may find yourself with few listeners.

Chicken Ranches

Many people think that the whole point of social media is to have as many contacts as possible. To that end, they engage in contact-mill behavior; what I have affectionately coined *chicken ranches*.

Gathering a large following may feed your ego, but you will soon find that many of these cheaply gathered followers don't care nuts about what you are doing. They aren't interested in promoting you; they all want to promote themselves!

If you think you can "win" at this game by plumping up your lists artificially, you won't have the best social media experience. This kind of misguided behavior reminds me of grade school popularity contests, but how loyal or interested can you expect these casual contacts to be?

Pecking Order

Preening your feathers in front of your flock is guaranteed to irritate them. Branding doesn't mean that you are establishing your superiority or dominance in your field. Good branding allows others to identify you with your work, and establishes a ready image for others to call to mind when they have a need for your product or services.

Uninformed marketing mavens from the old advertising paradigm often confuse social media with Hollywood. Your challenge in social media is to have real interaction with your followers. It's not about having the most fans or followers; it's about real conversations between equals.

On social media, there is a give and take between you and another; you are satellites around each other. Just like the game you used to play on the playground: hold your playmate's hands and spin around in a circle. If one lets go, both fall. Each person in this game is equally important.

Boneless Chicken Farms[1]

Some social-media-maven wannabes steal content from others without giving credit or links back to the content originator. I've had people steal articles, content, and images from me. This spineless behavior doesn't belong in a community where each individual's content, reputation, and originality is their currency.

---

1   *Boneless Chicken Farm* is the title of one of my favorite Gary Larson cartoons.

Cold-Hacked Chicken

I find typos and hasty misreads a source of unending amusement. A few years ago my older sister and I had the habit of eating at a local Chinese restaurant. One dish on the menu, entitled "Cold-Hacked Chicken," always mystified me: it seemed to imply something rather sinister on the part of the chef. That same week we found the companion dishes *Sordid Vegetables* and *Fisherman's Bladder.*[2]

My point is that on a platform with the global reach of Twitter and Linked In, you have to be both more culturally sensitive, and more culturally forgiving than ever before. You can commit social (media) gaffes just as easily as anyone else. Remember one person's *Cold-Hacked Chicken* may be someone else's *Sordid Vegetables.*

---

2   *Assorted Vegetables and Fisherman's Platter*

Chapter 6
—the social media citizen—

A Gathering of Birds

One could say that social media has created a new global community that transcends borders. This community is a nation of people who adhere to an unspoken etiquette or community ethics.

Self-expression, Conversation, Equality, Transparency, Community

At the base of these ethics is an understanding of the basic needs of the human individual who has chosen to live inside that community. The individual needs to be recognized by the community, and allowed free expression. To be counted by his peers as a good citizen of that community he adheres to the unspoken ethics of that community—respecting others as equals, partaking in conversations, and transparency in all his actions.

The person who stands to benefit most from social media is someone who can understand and use the five unique social media principles: self-expression, conversation, equality, transparency, and community.

In other words, you benefit from the medium because it suits your needs as much as the people you are communicating with. Because you are not trying to do any old-paradigm exploitation of the medium and its inhabitants, they will accept you as one of them, a person of like-mind whom they trust.

Extrapolating from these five principles: self-expression, conversation, equality, transparency, and community, we can form a picture of who stands to benefit most from social media:

1. Those who need to express themselves.

2. People who appreciate self-expression.

3. Those who need to share information.

Social media beneficiaries

- Writers
- Artists
- Educators
- Media and content producers
- Consultants
- Community-dependent venues
- Small businesses with unique offerings

- Businesses with niche markets
- Political figures
- Public Relation departments
- Educators
- Corporations and organizations

The best way for an individual to use social media is for self-expression, communication, and branding. The best use of social media for large organizations is education, communication, public service, community outreach, and customer service. The main thing is honesty in all communications: transparency will become the name of the game.

As people become more used to instant information on a grassroots level, dishonesty will become more easily discerned. Once an entity or a person is known to be dishonest, their reputation will be hard to regain.

The people who have the hardest time with social media are those who try to monetize it, and try to trick people into becoming fans, friends, or followers or mislead them with false information.

If a Bird Sings in the Wilderness...

The power of one—the social media individual
In our race to market to the masses (the old outdated consumerism model) or gain new followers (social media), we may forget that all groups are made up of individuals.

Social media is not about marketing to featureless crowds, but about communicating with groups of individuals, who hold certain interests in common with you.

Human have needs too...
Individuals like to be recognized, they like to talk with others like them. Social media takes advantage of a few basic human needs: to be valued, to converse, to help others, and to gather in groups of like-minded individuals.

These basic human needs have not been addressed by the advertising, corporate-consumer culture. That is why this phenomenon is so powerful and that is why it's called social media. Ignore this basic truth and you will not be successful on this platform.

The social media individual represents

- Individuality
- Personality
- Special interests

The social media individual needs

- To be recognized
- To be equal
- To be valued
- To converse
- To find a family of like individuals
- To be part of a community

Bird Tribes

The individuals on social media platforms are all part of other groups. Visualize this as a large field of individuals that you can gather into groups based upon similar characteristics: the people who like football can form one group, the ones who wear pink shirts can form another, those who eat cooked carrots are another.

Crossover interests create new groups
Some of the pink shirts may also eat cooked carrots. If you are initially part of a group that writes about their pink shirts, and you are getting their messages, you may find that they also recommend eating carrots, which you didn't think to research at first, but now you can follow whomever they follow as well.

One Hysterical Parrot

My brother has a parrot he inherited from his mother-in-law. I swear that it has a sense of humor. If you tell it to play dead, it lies down on its back and twitches theatrically in frantic death-throes. It likes to terrify the family dogs by chasing them out from under the couch. If you dare to sing near it, it will try to drown you out with an ear-splitting operatic aria.

Like my brother's parrot, social media mavens are intelligent, fun-loving individuals. They love:

- Humor
- Gossip
- Useful information
- Quotes
- Choice
- Links to more information
- Cleverness
- Succinctness
- Relevance
- Defined focus
- A community of like souls
- Originality

Bird Talk

The whole point of social media is interaction and conversation. When two or more individuals are gathered in the same space, conversation may ensue. When these people share interests, interesting conversation may result.

When the conversationalists start to share leads, contacts, or are able to help each other, conversation has a chance to become something more: a relationship. The goal of professional social media is to sponsor healthy relationships between colleagues, between a professional and her client, and between a company and a customer.

Before I created my first group on Linked In, I joined groups that paralleled my interests, started discussions, answered questions, and requested connections with members of the groups who interested me. I could pose a discussion in a group in search of information or leads for my work. One should not misuse a group to flagrantly market something, even yourself. Remember to share and to bring value to others in all your interactions.

I found my experience with groups working to my advantage when I created my first group on Linked In, "Caffeinated Creatives." As the author of several books on creativity and creative development, I felt that there wasn't really a group on Linked In that gave creative people a place to meet and help each other. I formed this group to mirror my interest in creativity and to meet the needs of creative people like myself.

As the leader of this group, I am careful to make sure that the members are protected from overt marketing attempts in the discussion groups and that everyone in the group has a positive, enriching and online experience. The discussion area on Linked In is the core of any group, so good, pertinent discussions that invite member participation and give information or help is key to maintaining a happy group.

The experience of leading this group has allowed me to experience being a lateral leader: my ideas and discussions are no more important than the ideas and discussions of anyone else in the group.

Birds of a Feather...

Individuals in social media mean nothing without a group with which to interact. The structure of social media is like a large party, the idea is not to just stand in the corner by yourself: you want to engage with others, meet them, talk, and see if you have similar interests in common.

You will naturally find some conversations more interesting than others. You will find groups of people who are gathered and who are holding a conversation on a shared interest.

If you think you have something to contribute, you may join the conversation; perhaps you will find a job, or a lead to a new business idea. Anything can happen if you are open and are willing to share knowledge, links, and contacts.

Before I created my first group on Linked In, I joined groups that paralleled my interests, started discussions, answered questions, and requested connections with members of the groups who interested me. I could pose a discussion in a group in search of information for my work.

One cannot misuse this opportunity to flagrantly market something, even yourself, or you may find your messages flagged, or you may be even thrown out of the group. Remember to share and to bring value to others in all your interactions.

I found my experience with groups working to my advantage when I created my first group on Linked In, that I called Creative Caffeine. As the author of several books on creativity and creative development, I felt that there wasn't really a group on Linked In that gave creative people a place to meet, and help each other. I formed this group to mirror my interest in creativity and to meet the needs of creative people like myself.

As the leader of this group, I am careful to make sure that the members are protected from overt marketing attempts in the discussion groups and that everyone in the group has a positive, enriching online experience. The discussion area on Linked In is the core of any group, so good, pertinent discussions that invite member participation and give information or help is key to maintaining a happy group.

Leading this group has allowed me to experience being a lateral leader: my ideas and discussions are no more important than the ideas and discussions of anyone else in the group. I can see how popular my thoughts are by the natural selection of the group. The group "votes" on the most interesting discussions posted by members of the group by their participation.

Chapter 7

—branding is not advertising—

Bird Song

As a tool for communication and self-expression on a global scale, nothing beats social media. Here is a break down of how to best use this tool.

Professional Credentials
You can use social media to communicate your knowledge on a subject, and establish yourself as an authority in your field. Having a blog on your topic may be a great way to get your next job in that area.

Communication/Customer service
Social media can serve as your front line of communicating with your current clients/customers or with potential ones.

Branding
Branding is a great way to use social media, but it is not to be confused with advertising. Branding is basically a way to establish an image in someone's mind about who you are and what you represent. It is very useful for public figures as well as businesses. Branding on social media is not to be confused with advertising, and combines the two former points: establishing credentials, and communication.

Public Relations

Keeping abreast of your online reputation is a skill of conversation rather than branding. This is a perfect way for companies and public figures to interface with their customers and fans. As stated by Doc Searls and David Wagner, two authorities on the effects of Internet on marketing, advertising, and PR,

"The best of the people in PR are not PR types at all. They understand that there aren't censors, they're the company's best conversationalists." Social media provides an environment where users and PR professionals can converse, and where PR professionals can promote their brand and improve their company's image by listening and responding to what the public is saying about their product.[3]

Education

A businessperson may need to show how their product can or should be used. This is an excellent use of social media. Susan Riehle of Studio Productions, Inc. sells special effects product used in theatrical productions to make people and objects appear and disappear on stage. Not surprisingly, a product like this requires

---

3—http://en.wikipedia.org/wiki/Social_media

understanding of the lighting techniques involved. A product like hers benefits greatly from the YouTube videos on how to use these beautiful theatrical scrims. These movies don't sell the product; they just simply explain how to use them.

Content Creation

Just as television turned a nation of people who listened to media content into watchers of media content, the emergence of social media has created a nation of media content creators. According to 2011 Pew Research data, nearly 80% of American adults are online and nearly 60% of them use social networking sites.

More Americans get their news via the Internet than from newspapers or radio, as well as three-fourths who say they get news from e-mail or social media sites updates, according to a report published by CNN. The survey suggests that Facebook and Twitter make news a more participatory experience than before as people share news articles and comment on other people's posts. According to CNN, in 2010 75% of people got their news forwarded through e-mail or social media posts, while 37% of people shared a news item via Facebook or Twitter.

Bird Watching

OK, I might lose you here. I'm going to use some *Marketing-Speak*. But hang in with me, you can do this, and your business, cause, communications, and relationships will improve immensely as a result.

The following is the quick way to arrive at a reasonable idea of the message you are trying to communicate and the brand or idea that you want to embody. You might want to go the official route and engage the services of your neighborhood public relations expert, agent, graphic designer, or advertising firm after you do this preliminary exercise, but it is a good thing to do in any event.

-:-:-:-:-

Mission/Vision statement

When public relations or marketing people want to promote a brand or a person, they first try to determine what that person or brand is; they make a portrait of the brand. You can arrive at a mission/vision statement by examining just what you want to do and why you want to do it. What benefits to others does your work provide? Your mission/vision statement is what you want to do, how you do it, and what your mission/business/cause will provide for others.

First know who you are
It might seem silly, but most of us never learn to define who and what we are, and what we are bringing to the table. To promote yourself, whether writing a resume or creating a new world order, you have to first know who you are.

I recommend that you take a few minutes to develop a personal vision / mission statement. Here's how to develop a personal vision/mission statement.

STEP 1—Think about what is important to you.

What makes you feel fulfilled and happy? Make a list of these things.

STEP 2—List your strengths.

Now combine these two lists and extrapolate a statement of who you are, what you bring to others and what you want to bring to the world. This is your Self Definition.

STEP 3—Envision your perfect life.

Be as specific as possible: where do you want to live, who do you live with, what do you want to be doing? Don't be afraid to dream big: this is brainstorming! It is important at this stage not to limit your imagination (or yourself).

STEP 4 (optional)—list what you don't like about your life as it is now.

If you are having problems creating positive scenarios, then write down, by way of contrast, a list of what is NOT working in your life on the left side of a piece of paper. Draw a line down the middle of the sheet of paper and write down the positive opposite of each point on the right side. Now that you know what you want, you can stop focusing on what you don't want and focus instead on what you DO want.

STEP 5—Now describe your perfect life again.

Now write a paragraph of the life you want, in the present tense, as if you are already living it.

-:-:-:-:-

Another way to fly

Here's an exercise you may find useful: take a sheet of paper. divide it down the middle, and put what you want to do on the left side and what you think people need on the right side. Don't bother relating one to the other; just let the thoughts flow.

Then draw lines connecting the phrases that match each other: you are matching your talents/desires on one side with the needs/desires of your clients on the other. Now, using your best high-school English, you can combine the paragraphs and phrases into a reasonable mission/vision statement. Don't worry; it isn't a test, so it doesn't have to be perfect. It just has to make sense to you. The mission/vision statement is why you do what you do; maybe it's even why you get up every morning.

How to brand yourself, your cause, or your company

All marketers make a portrait of the brand they are marketing. Think about who you want to be to others. What is the image you want to come to your client's minds when they think of you. It's your portrait in the mirror.

Clay Birds

Marketing 101 for Self-Promotion
Whether you are simply applying for a job or starting a new company, basic marketing principles still apply. If you haven't already, go to earlier articles on this blog to complete your vision/mission statement and life plan. Now that you know who you are and what you offer, use the following basic questions to help you focus your marketing efforts:

Who is your target market? Even if you are a job seeker, it is a good idea to make a portrait of your client. Say you are looking for a job as an IT tech; it would be a good idea to use keywords in your resume that pertain to those interests. You will be writing your resume to appeal to your ideal employer (target market), use his language; make sure you write your resume to fit his expectations. A good deal of marketing depends upon an accurate portrait of the target client. You have to match your ad to the expectations of the potential client, otherwise you will have lost him before you can even get your message heard.

What product or service are you offering? This involves knowing yourself. Only offer what you want to do, not just your past experience, otherwise you might find yourself in an unhappy position. If you know what your target wants you can figure out how to offer it to them I like to ask the Who, What, Why, and How questions to help me define the brand.

- WHAT are you offering?

- WHY are people going to buy from you?

- WHY you and not someone else?

- WHAT distinguishes you from others?

- WHAT is your brand?

- HOW is your product/service different?

- HOW are you going to deliver it?

Defining these things helps you know how to present yourself, your product, or your business. A marketing plan can just fall into place.

Social media modules

Following are some social media modules and social media support structures that you may want to build. Every one of these items has to updated and maintained, so be discerning about what you put online. If you can't manage it yourself, hire someone who can.

WEBSITE

Technically, websites are not classified as social media, but they can function that way. A website is an essential part of almost any business nowadays.

If you are a business, spend your money on the best design you can get. If you are a personality, or want to be, get a website with a domain name the same as your name. If you aren't a personality or business, skip the website, don't pass GO, don't collect $100, and get a blog instead.

-:-:-:-:-

Do You Really Need That Website?

I have been a designer in the web-space for a long time. I have seen the web go from being a simple text string on a browser window to a complex visual design. I was part of the dot com bubble in New York City, and personally witnessed it bursting a couple years later.

People would come to me to design their website. Sometimes I would tell them that they didn't need one, or that they could be just as happy with a cheap template. Why do a custom design for a simple site? Custom design is simply too expensive for most folks at a minimum of $3000 for a well-designed site.

Without a doubt websites have become an indispensable tool in contemporary culture. I now think that everyone doing any kind of business should have one, and perhaps every individual should too.

The caveat is that if you want to skimp on good (graphic) design, it would be far better to have no site at all. A badly designed website—and any other marketing materials—will hurt your image far more than you probably realize.

A website is only one item in your package of marketing materials. A website alone is not enough—you should support it with your business card, your brochure, your profile on Linked In, your blog, newsletter, and so forth.

BLOG

- Choose a niche, not something too broad.
- You should update your blog at least every week.

- The blog can be fed into your website
- Connect your blog to other social media

-:-:-:-:-

Blog Your Way to Success

Blogs and social networking establish you as an authority. With the power of the word, you can get new customers, build your business, establish your reputation, and sell your product or service.

Why bother creating a website when a blog will do? Search Engines search text, not images. Design appeals to the customer, but it is text that the search engine indexes so that your customer can find you. Whatever other marketers will tell you, you can't fool Mother Nature or the Search Engine Spiders for long. T

hey know when they are slammed with copy that is keyword-rich, but content-poor. Write relevant copy for your readers on a subject that interests you. If your blog is to support your business you might want to hire a professional writer to write articles for you. That way, you can focus on your business knowing that the search engines are finding you through the fresh content that you are posting regularly.

NEWSLETTER

- Write on what you know.
- Your newsletter can be set to deliver your blog's content whenever you post.
- Do not spam people and don't buy lists.
- Add people only when they know what they are getting (double opt-in).
- Target your newsletter's content to your topic.

LINKED IN

- For professional networking.
- Request connections with new people and old contacts.
- Build your profile with your brand and your slogan.
- Ask for clients to write you testimonials.
- Join groups.
- Answer questions.
- Start a group of your own.

TWITTER

- Twitter is a micro-blogging platform.
- Build your profile with your brand and your slogan.

- Appropriate for brief announcements, customer service, making connections.
- Update at least 3 times per week.

AUDIO/VIDEO
- Post videos on YouTube or Vimeo
- Build a "channel" with a unique name, a "brand" that defines the content
- Include on blogs, websites, etc.
- Connect (embed) the video into Twitter, websites, Linked In, etc.

Who is your client?

Even if you are just working with social media to build your personal and professional reputation, so you can get a job at the local Burgers-R-Us, you should know whom you want to talk to—i.e. your client, your future boss, or your future customers. This is what professional marketers do, and while this book basically eschews marketing techniques in the social media arena, this one is an essential lesson from the marketing pundits.

Here's how it works: copy the needs/desires of your potential clients from the mission/vision exercise above—if you are like me, you tried to cheat by doing it in your head, so do it now—paste them into a new document, and like a detective at a crime scene, make a portrait of the client from the clues you have in front of you.

This exercise should bring a great deal of clarity to your social media campaign if you have been having problems. Remember, we are not using social media to market products or services; we are using it to establish our reputation and our brand, create relationships, and spark conversations between our associates.

How Do You Package Yourself?

Many people make the mistake of assuming that creativity or originality is what sells. This is not true. If it were, people would be buying original paintings instead of cheap reproductions. They would value a hand-knitted sweater over a cashmere name brand. Instead, people have values that restrain them to the known, to what other people value, to what makes them look good, and to what is useful to them.

A client of mine revealed that she was concerned about what exactly she was selling. I realized that she is ready to market herself, but like many of us has trepidations about committing herself to her path. The excuse that she is using to keep herself from moving forward is that she doesn't have a product or service that is exclusively hers. This is just an excuse: after all, how many products out there are truly original or exclusive? New companies would have a very hard time starting for tripping over all the trademarks and patents out there.

And how does one reconcile monetary success with following one's heart: doing what one loves? I know many artists who do what they love and make not one penny from their art.

All else being equal, what is it that makes one idea successful and another not? It boils down to one thing: the packaging. In the final analysis, content is not what sells a product: the packaging is what sells. I am not suggesting that one should not provide good quality, but no matter the quality of your product, if you do not know your customer, you do not know how to present your content in a way he can value.

Like a good date or marriage, you and your potential customer are in a relationship. You can paint a portrait of your ideal client, you know him so well. Thus, you know what he prefers in the way of imagery, colors, words, style, and the "look and feel" of the design.

These qualities are what a good graphic designer can define: every communication, publication, brochure, press release, and website should adhere to the communication style and preferences of your consumer. In order to effectively self-promote, you have to create a package that is you. It is not important that you be original—although great original packaging is worth its weight in gold— think of the countless jean brands out there.

What sells the high-priced designer brand over the low-priced generic? One part is the design of the clothes, but what makes the clothes "visible" to the harried customer—who admittedly has so many other brands to choose from—is the successful image imparted in the advertising. It is the packaging or marketing that really sells a product..

In deciding how you are going to package yourself, your product or your service, it is important that you know your client and how what you do coincides with that client's hopes and desires. A good graphic designer can match the design and text with that client's style of communication, preferences and secret dreams. How well you match these will determine, to a large degree, the success of your product or service.

Your slogan

From my mouth to your ear, a slogan is a quick, catchy, text version of your sound byte (see below). If it is short enough, you can use it in your Linked In and Twitter profiles, as well as on your website and blog.

Your sound bite

The sound byte is the synopsis of what you do in a short sentence. Also called the elevator pitch, in the old days it was fast enough to be shoveled in your ear in the time it took the elevator to go to the next floor by a furtive MAD man in a narrow-lapelled suit. In the era of social media the sound byte has evolved to a super-abbreviated quip: think Tweet.

Designing Your Slogan or Sound Bite

When people ask you what you do, do you stammer and hesitate? A ready reply can be your ticket to your success. Your slogan and your sound bite can be every bit as important as your business card or website.

How do you make one? Think about yourself from your customer's standpoint. What benefit do you bring them?

Say you are a personal trainer. I know a trainer who calls himself the "Zen Commando." His name says it all. He was in the war, and trained commandos. Now he trains San Diegans as if they were in the army. He looks the part too, bulging chest muscles under a vest is his standard issue. He hosts a boot camp on the beach, and charges over $150.00 for an hour of training with him.

Someone else I know brands herself as the "Water Queen." She believes in the water ionizer that she sells, and has no problem telling everyone she meets that she is the queen of water.

It is important to believe in what you are doing. Your integrity and passion for your product is what sells. People buy because they believe in you, therefore a salesperson that believes in their product is bound to be successful. Your slogan is a summation of who you are to your potential client. It should reflect your beliefs, brand you, and help you market your services, all at the same time.

A good slogan, like a good business name, is priceless because it is an indispensable item in your branding and promotion program.

Chapter 8
—in a niche all your own—

Homing Pigeons Always Fly Home

Small niches and special interest groups
A family is a natural group formation, but people are social beings, and will naturally gather in groups outside their families and nations.

How do people form voluntary groups? One way is by defining interests they hold in common; the result is a Special Interest Group.

Wikipedia's definition of Special Interest Group

—a community with an interest in advancing a specific area of knowledge, learning or technology where members cooperate to effect or to produce solutions within their particular field, and may communicate, meet, and organize conferences.

They may at times also advocate or lobby on a particular issue or on a range of issues but are generally distinct from advocacy groups and pressure groups which are normally set up for the specific political aim; the distinction is not firm however and some organizations can adapt and change their focus over time.

Wikipedia's definition of niche market:

—the subset of the market on which a specific product is focusing; therefore the market niche defines the specific product features aimed at satisfying specific market needs, as well as the price range, production quality and the demographics that is intended to impact.

Simply stated, identifying, forming, and communicating to a SIG or niche market works very well on social media. One success story that I heard is the guy who sells crème brûlée from a street vending cart in San Francisco. He uses Twitter to announce his daily location to his loyal (and mobile) following. He sells out of product every day.

Another example of niche exploitation is the guy who writes independent reviews of fast food in New York City on his blog. He has a big following, and I'm sure he has enough SIG followers to be able to post ads from large advertisers on his blog. He has achieved independent success by writing about what he loves.

Find Your Flock

So how do you find your flock of people who think like you? First, extrapolate your interests from your mission statement. This will give you keywords that you can search online.

I researched individuals on Twitter and groups on Linked In that reflected my interests. When I found an individual on Twitter who interested me, I followed her, and looked to see if she had a list that reflected my interests. Following the individuals on that list helped me build my own flock; the individuals I found formed the basis of my own nascent lists.

I joined groups on Linked In, and monitored the discussions before I tried to participate. I waited even longer to start a new discussion of my own. You have to get a good idea of what the group is about before posting, and make sure you are adhering to the group rules and etiquette first, or you might get flagged.

The Twitter list is a group, like a petri dish, it is a collection of individual cells, grouped by familial similarities. On Linked In, this list is a group that you can join or create; your professional connections can be considered another list. On Facebook, this list is composed of your friends, or it can be a fan base, group, or cause.

I find now that others follow me, based upon my Tweets or Linked In discussions, and I am on several very interesting lists that others have formed. I review these lists that include my name: I find other interesting people to follow this way. I have my Twitter account set up to inform me when someone follows me. I look at their profile: if I am interested, I follow them back, and sometimes I write to them or retweet some of their more interesting comments.

I am not interested in following everyone and her sister: I am only interested in interesting people who bring value and originality to my conversations and interactions. On Linked In, I screen people who want to connect with me, and choose carefully those I invite to connect.

Several people who are Facebook fans have complained to me about the privacy policy on Linked In that restricts connection requests, but this is exactly why Linked In is an effective professional networking platform. If you were famous, would you want your privacy invaded by rabid fans or your email to be spammed with marketing ploys? Linked In promotes professional behavior. As a result, you are more likely to find better business connections on Linked In than on Facebook.

Remember on any social medium your professional image is online and potentially visible to the world. What face are you presenting online? I would recommend that anyone who wishes to be well known in any field to restrict their Facebook account to real family and friends.

A Bird in the Hand

The quality and precision of your list determines your effectiveness in the social media sphere. There are many people who don't know the value of establishing who they are, and defining their interests with razor precision. They follow others willy-nilly, and their followers, friends and connections show the same confusion and lack of quality as the items in a dollar store.

This idea is the core concept behind my think upside-down approach to social media: rather than gathering many cheap followers who have little or no interest in your conversation, contacts, links, ideas, information, skills, profile, cause, brand, or product; you choose to gather a few choice contacts that you assiduously nurture, feed, and help.

Choosing to market to a small group, rather than a big group, is called niche marketing. Social media allows you to take niche marketing one step further and form a relationship with your target market.

Earlier in this book, I defined social media as the anti-mass-marketing engine. There is at least one guy who agrees with me. Chris Guillebeau publishes a blog called "The Art of Non-Conformity." [4] He advocates the idea of marketing to a small, loyal clan, as opposed to trying to gather and market to the masses.

What Guillebeau has to say about small armies sums up a good social media practice. His contention is that it is better to have a few loyal followers who truly like what you do and who you are than a huge flock of flighty fans.

4   www.chrisguillebeau.com

Chapter 9

—using viral to your advantage—

Bird Flu

Marketing on social media is viral, grassroots, and above all, requires voluntary participation by the individuals in your flock.

There are no shortcuts in social media: you have to first gather your flock; you have to make sure you talk their language, and then give them what they want: information, links or contacts.

Just like the bird flu, social media is viral; in fact, social media platforms inadvertently provide the perfect environment for the growth and proliferation of viral marketing. But don't call it marketing and don't approach it as marketing (see "allergens" above). I am not saying that marketing doesn't have a place in your brand or cause, but that it has to be adapted for social media.

Feel-Good Marketing—Article 1

So, how can you market your product or service in the age of social media? In an era of user-generated media and citizen reporters, how can an honest company or service provider get their message across? Is advertising dead?

With the advent of citizen reportage and in an age when explosive viral media that can circle the globe with the click of a button, companies and marketers have to adapt their attitudes, and think of the consumer in a different way. I propose a radical shift that I call "feel-good marketing."

Here are a few simple guidelines:

1. Make it easy for them to buy your product— remove the obstacles to sale

2. Make your product stand out as the clear choice in a sea of choices

3. Inspire confidence in your company with professional design and branding

4. Show your product in terms of its value to your consumer

5. Understand your customer's motivations

6. Make them feel good about their choice

7. Offer them a chance to "do good"

Speaking from a designer's point of view, the art of marketing is a matter of branding, image and point of sale. The science of marketing is best left to those who study the analytics.

This article is about how and why people buy, and specifically the less obvious motivators in current trends. I will focus on the guidelines listed above, meanwhile expanding on the definition of feel-good marketing.

Here is one definition: "Feel Good marketing involves promoting products that make people feel good about themselves because they are helping to make a better world for all."[5]

Now, a company that only does this kind of feel-good marketing may fail because it is not watching the bottom line, or because the primary motivator is lacking: "how does buying this item benefit me?" The

---

5   Steve Gillich CTM, President of the Canadian Institute of Travel Counselors

company may fail because they did not fulfill one or more of the other guidelines listed above.

A broader definition of feel-good marketing is that the customer should feel good about buying your product/service from the start of the buying process to the sale, and through the life of that product/service as well. Every businessman knows that repeat customers are the best customers. A repeat customer is one who has had a positive experience with the company.

A company should be concerned with customer retention, through a sustained positive experience. They might have sold me something once, but I won't continue or buy again if I have a negative experience. Worse, through viral marketing, a disgruntled consumer has ever more power to affect other people's opinions than before. Each step in the marketing guidelines outlined above can be seen in terms of feel-good marketing:

1. Make it easy for potential customers to buy your product—remove the obstacles to the sale

This is best done by good design: if on the Internet, make the path to the sale obvious and intuitive to your buyer. Give him access to plenty of rationale to back up his decision to buy your product, not in the top level of the site architecture where it may confuse him, but in the lower levels. Other media has to be even clearer and succinct.

A user feels good about the buying process because it is easy and clear. The last thing you want to do is to confuse him with too much information, clutter, and lack of information hierarchy. If the potential buyer is confused, he feels stupid, and is much less willing to buy.

2. Make your product stand out as the clear choice in a sea of choices

Again, this is the job of the designer. A good designer makes the value of the brand clear to the consumer. Even if the brand is more expensive than the competition, the user feels good about buying this product over another. The direct benefit of buying a brand has to be clear. Why would a person buy designer jeans when any pair has the same function?

3. Inspire confidence in your company with professional design and branding

Building an image is a careful process of using good design to inspire confidence and trust in a company. Customers buy for many reasons, but once a fly-by-night-here-today-gone-tomorrow company has burned them, they are cautious of trusting their money to unprofessional-looking businesses.

4. Show your product in terms of its value and benefits to your customer

This is the same as in point #2: the customer has to be sure of how the product is going to benefit them. They naturally want to feel good about the value of the product they are thinking of buying.

5. Understand your customer

A good designer and marketer knows how to paint the "portrait" of the target consumer, so that she can target her design or marketing to the needs and desires of that consumer.

Understanding what motivates someone to buy your product is a key part of the early design and marketing process. One of the prime motivations is the desire to feel good about not just what they purchase, but about themselves as a consumer.

6. Make your customer feel good about their choice post sale

Make them feel smart, and savvy through good customer service, and support. The repeat customer and longtime client is your best, least expensive form of advertising (see my articles on viral marketing and community building). Nonexistent or poor customer service is a form of very expensive negative advertising for your business.

I predict that, in the near future, companies will rise and fall due to the power of the consumer and buzz marketing. Make sure that the word out on the street about you is not negative. In addition, you can support your customers with social media: communicate with them, respond to their questions, and allow them to become your advocates.

7. Offer them a chance to do-good

Lastly, although this is not a prime motivator for most people, it will be an incredible boost to your company if you can offer your consumers a way to feel through altruistic action. Make it easy for them to "do right" and to feel that their purchase, although made primarily for their own benefit, can do something for others or for the environment. In this way, people can feel good about being part of a larger community of people.

-:-:-:-:-

Feel Good Marketing—Article 2

In the first article on Feel Good Marketing, I talked about how a company can get and retain customers by generating a "feel good" experience for the consumer throughout the entire business process; from marketing, through the sale, through post sale, and for the life of the product.

I recounted an example of poor customer service by way of example of how a company may be able to sell a customer on their product, but fall down during the post sale experience. As a balance, I want to show a couple of examples of how a company can do well through the entire process.

Recently, I bought a new cell phone with Virgin Mobile and had a great experience with this company. I'll go though the principles above, one by one, to see how Virgin Mobile has racked up a 10 in my scoring system so far.

1. Remove the obstacles to the sale—make it easy for people to buy your product

Virgin Mobile has a variety of phones in Target, a place where I shop for a variety of other things. The packaging allows me to see that the process looks easy, and I have a good range of choices, but not so many that I feel confused.

The process was clear: buy the phone and follow the easy instructions inside the brochure. The distressed typeface and red/black/white color scheme is not exactly easy to read, but it fits the company's young image.

2. Make your product stand out as the clear choice in a sea of choices

I had a variety of choices in Target. No other company offered the camera phone I wanted at such a low cost as Virgin Mobile. The other pre-paid companies didn't have the coverage of Virgin Mobile (which uses the Sprint network), or they had expensive phones.

3. Inspire confidence in your company with professional design and branding

The image of the company is that of a hip young alternative to the expensive post-paid phones. When you call them to set up the phone, a young girl called Simone answers. The voice is not that of the bland vanilla corporate voice mail operator, but someone you or I might already know.

Although, I got pretty tired of Simone's patter after trying to get to a live operator for a couple of days, still I appreciated her friendly tone and verbiage, even when told I had to wait yet again.

4. Show your product in terms of its value and benefits to your customer

The brochure made it clear that I could control my costs easily, without overage charges. The camera phone was only $59, as opposed to a comparable AT&T phone at over $200.00.

5. Understand your customer

The copy on the brochure and packaging was targeted directly to someone like me, who has been burned by post-paid charges (I once had a $700. bill with a cell phone service) and wants to not only keep their costs down, but keep their current number and have flexible plans.

6. Make them feel good about their choice

Now, this gets interesting. I had a problem switching my phone number from my former cell phone service to Virgin Mobile. I started the process with a call on Friday; the issue was not resolved until the following Tuesday.

For an entire day, I made calls between the two companies, trying to resolve the problem; I started to feel like a Ping-Pong ball in a match. Until that day, I had been very happy with my old service, and I had made a point of telling them so. The tech people had been very helpful, and I liked being able to have a phone service without a contract.

As the day wore on, I contemplated what it would mean to me to lose this number. I was finally resigned to my loss, but by 10 p.m. that night, I got a message from Virgin Mobile that I had retained the number.

I was surprised, and pleased. I am not clear who it was that actually achieved this feat. I would like to thank whoever it was. However, my point is that during this process I got to talk quite a bit to the people at Virgin Mobile, especially Ron, the manager.

Ron told me that he, himself, has a Virgin Mobile cell phone and is pleased with it. He started to outline some of the features that are not apparent at first glance. Some of these appealed a great deal to me, such as the ability to switch on the fly between plans. For instance, if you are on a monthly plan, and want to go on vacation, you can switch to a pre-paid until you get back. Ron made me feel that I had made the right choice to buy from a company that not only offers me the kind of flexibility I desire, but good, knowledgeable customer service; people who were willing to go out of their way to help me.

Most companies do not sufficiently reward good employees who go the extra mile for their customers. Perhaps they don't understand the first two principles of business: 1.) The satisfied customer is your best advertisement, and 2.) The customer you already have is your best customer. Retaining that customer saves the cost of going out and getting a new customer. A happy customer does your advertising for you.

Consumers should report when they are well served by someone in customer service, to thank these front-line employees when they do a good job—sometimes despite company regulations. Customer service employees often are not paid well enough; after all, they take a lot of flak in the name of the company.

7. Offer them a chance to do-good

During the many calls I made to Virgin Mobile, the hold contained a message from Jewel about the many homeless kids on the street, and about Virgin Mobile's effort to give phones to them. The package the phone came in contained a postage paid envelope for shipping used phones to the company for recycling or as gifts to the homeless. I used the package to mail my used phone (good riddance!) to Virgin Mobile.

The entire process of buying from Virgin Mobile makes me feel good: I feel good that I made a good purchase. I got exactly what I wanted: I kept my number, I got the phone I wanted, and I have a flexible plan with a company that provides excellent customer support. Best of all, Virgin Mobile helped me do-good by recycling my old phone by giving it to the homeless.

Feel Good Marketing—Article 3

This last article on feel-good marketing focuses on customer service: that part of the company that most advertisers and marketers seem to ignore. It is, admittedly, the hardest part of any business. Sales/customer service is the front line of any business, and it merits a great deal of attention.

Since your service people represent your company, it is imperative that they do a good job. There are several ways to ensure this: good training, good pay, perks, benefits, a reliable support system from the company to back them up, and innovative ways to relieve the inevitable stress of dealing with customers all day.

Allow them some latitude in dealing with the customers, something that they can provide (a benefit to the customer, monetary benefit, reimbursement of fees paid, etc.) to ensure that the customer walks away with a positive experience.

Above all, let them know when they have done a good job. Give them promotions, time off, or other perks at that time, let them know that their feedback is appreciated, and you take their view seriously.

As a consumer, and commentator on corporate culture, I make sure that the manager of a good customer service representative knows when they have done a good job. The customer service employee represents your company to the customer. Treat him/her well because it is these people who can make or break your business.

When a customer has a positive experience with your company, they are likely to talk about it. Through viral marketing, your company is advertised for free.

Long-term, word of mouth is the cheapest form of marketing there is. Viral marketing is very active online in various forms of social media.

The key to viral marketing is the recommendation of one customer to another. Traditional advertising is a whole lot more expensive. One positive experience may translate to a lot more customers and more business, depending on the reach of that customer. A smart business makes sure that the customers have positive experiences with the company; viral media helps them leverage this to gain more customers.

Viral marketing only works if the word out on the street about you is good, and that is the lesson: use feel good marketing throughout your entire business process, from advertising to customer service. And don't forget to support your employees.

-:-:-:-:-

Sales Principles at the Heart of Good Marketing

- Know your product / service.

- Know the needs of your customer.

- Give them exactly what they need now, and for their future needs.

- Present the features (and limitations) of every item/service you sell clearly, so the user can make an informed decision.

- Assist the customer in making the right decision for them, even if you send them elsewhere.

- Educate the customer on their purchase—now and in the future.

- Allow them as much follow-up as needed for them to enjoy their purchase.

- Allow them to return their purchase

- Allow the customer a way to share your passion for your product or service with others.

- Always consider the customer a long-term client, and think first of him, rather than of the individual sale.

Flying Tips

To sum up, below are some pithy tips and tricks for becoming a social media magnet, maven, and magnate without losing too much sleep on those red-eye flights.

Make Yourself a Magnet for Others

What do you represent? How do you differentiate yourself, your brand, and your business from the rest of the flock? You are a magnet for others when you are true to yourself, when you are clear about what you offer, and when you offer conversations and information of value to your flock.

Quality Over Quantity

No matter who you are or what you produce, this new age requires quality in all that you do. Give value, give information, give help, and give freely.

Branding Without Advertising

Branding = good. Advertising = bad. No one wants to be marketed to these days. They want information so they can make informed decisions. Good branding can represent you in a way that people can easily identify who you are and what you represent.

The Art of Conversation

You wouldn't go to a party of geeks and talk about breeding turtles, would you? It's not enough to gather a flock of interested and interesting people. Remember to feed your flock the food that they like.

Customer Service

Business on social media is not business as usual. In the age of viral communication that started with email and has culminated in the evolution of social media, business has to be responsible and responsive to the customer, to the environment, and to society at large.

Managing Your Content and Your Life

Don't' allow social media to run your life. Participate in only the platforms and discussions that interest you. Remember that you don't have to follow anyone else's rules, even the ones I have outlined in this book. Do it your own way: think upside-down in every part of your life. It will make you happier and will make your life so much more interesting.

Cross-Pollinate Your Social Media

There are some amazing online resources that enable you to lessen the work you have to do to promote, brand, and communicate online.

These change daily, but two I recommend are Hootsuite and Wordpress. Hootsuite will allow you to schedule posts weeks in advance, and cross-post to other Twitter accounts, Facebook, Linked In, and other social media platforms.

Wordpress has become the platform of choice for both blogging and instant websites. There are a lot of third-party vendors of plugins that make your online life more efficient. Wordpress includes a lot of cross-distribution tools embedded in the software that allow you to post automatically to other platforms such as Facebook and Twitter.

Another great tool is MailChimp, which gives you the tools to create, grow, and maintain a double opt-in mailing list. Using RSS, you can instruct MailChimp to pick up each new article that you post on your blog or Wordpress self-hosted website, and email it automatically as a newsletter to your list.

And, finally, I would recommend checking out cloud services, which allow you to store and share files remotely. I have run huge collaborative projects from a cloud service. If you don't find these particular services that I have recommended above, then search for their parallels; these things evolve rapidly.

Know the Definition of True Wealth

You can start to look at your contacts, your conversations, and your relationships as your true wealth. In the process of building your virtual network, don't forget that you have real family and friends. Spend time with them.

Chapter 10
—living the good life—

The Tools That Shape Us

I like to reflect on the evolution of science, technology and human culture. As a cultural observer and somewhat jaded technologist, I find it interesting to observe how technology affects us.

When I was in the 6th grade I was addicted to science fiction. I once read a short story that I now see as an allegory for how the tools that we make shape us.

A group of scientists had invented a time machine, and were testing it, putting objects in the machine and sending them back in time. They sent hammers back to the Stone Age and radios back to the American Revolution. But no matter what they did, nothing seemed to change, so they thought their machine had failed.

However, as they threw each object into the machine, the bodies of the scientists slowly changed: their arms became more like tentacles, and their faces developed multiple eyes. Their technology was inexorably changing them, even though, from their standpoint, they couldn't see what was happening.

Like the time machine in the story, I think that the tools that we create and use shape our culture, our communications, and in some cases, even ourselves. But like the scientists in the story, we cannot see how the tools are changing us, and, because we don't know what is happening, we cannot control what is happening to us.

The lure of technology creates a cultural blindness. People get lost in the tool and can't see the bigger picture. Do you know that in the Renaissance, oil paint and Italian perspective were cutting edge technologies? These were revolutionary technologies in those days. But when you see a great painting from that period—say the Mona Lisa—do you think of the oil paint or of the painting?

Technology is important only in when it works well. The artists in the Renaissance who used the cutting edge technology of the day experimented with it, and sometimes they failed; most of da Vinci's "Last Supper" fell off the wall because he tried to combine oil paint with water-based fresco. But when an artist had the idea of combining the egg tempera of the former age with the (then) modern medium of oil paint, he was successful. This new "mixed technique" resulted in some of the most long lasting and beautiful paintings ever produced.

As an artist, I am interested in culture, so I find it very interesting how our tools change us. Just think of the evolution of the button. It seems that the button started out in ancient Roman or Egyptian times as a type of clasp, perhaps to fasten a cloak. Later, in the pre-Industrial Age, people used buttons to fasten their ankle boots. They even used a tool to help them do this: a buttonhook. In the Machine Age, the button was used to start or connect electrical equipment.

CD ROM, early web, and kiosk interface design introduced the first virtual button: these graphics were made to look like a familiar mechanical or electrical button, so that people new to interactive design (everyone) would get the idea that they were supposed to "push" them. They were designed to look pushed in when on and even sometimes read "on" or "off" to indicate their state.

The pages on a contemporary website are connected together by the virtual button, just as the sides of one's nineteenth century shoes were fastened or brought together with the buttons of the day. This use of the familiar to introduce the new has psychological and practical ramifications for the savvy interface designer. This is how we advance culture, design, language and human interaction.

What is the similarity in all forms of the button from early prehistory to its current form—the function of the button has always been to "fasten" or "connect" two things together, whether it be the sides of your Roman homespun itchy wool cloak, or to bridge one webpage to another.

Today, buttons can be anything, and the audience has grown in sophistication with the designer. In effect, a good designer "teaches" the user what is interactive in a subtle manner. JavaScript introduced the "rollover" effect on the web, but it was first introduced years before on CD and on kiosks.

If you look at the technology of social media in the broadest terms, you can see how the effect of any technology can change us, can change our way of thinking, interacting, socializing—even our ethics and worldview. Perhaps we should choose how we want to change before we find ourselves changed without our permission.

Build Community

This new world is about community. Not just the community that you belong to, but more importantly, the community you are building. No longer do you have to fit into a structure that someone else has built, but you can build communities of your own.

A Community Starts With One

In this time of rapid technological advances and cultural change, a new standard of self-evaluation is needed. Perhaps, we can start basing our values upon more solid ground, and see that an individual's worth can no longer be based upon ephemeral things like his material possessions or even upon the experience that he has accrued; but upon his creativity, long-term relationships, and upon the reputation he has established among his peers.

The lessons of the phenomenon of social media go far beyond the tools, etiquette, or rewards. They represent a larger movement of people away from what I call the "hive mentality" of the corporate-controlled consumer nation-states, towards a greener, more human future, full of interesting ideas, creative solutions to global problems, jobs that make us feel good, and communities that serve all the members equally.

Regardless of how you decide to use social media, it is not good if you let it run your life. Technology is only a tool, not a source of freedom. And perhaps, after reading this book, you might want to step out all together and do something really new, something radically different.

-:-:-:-:-

The Beginning of the End of Time

What better time to build that new green business, meet new people, sail around the world, have a child, adopt a baby, take loving care of your elderly parents, start a new career, take up photography, make a movie, climb Mt Everest, learn to ski, go on a archeological dig, teach reading, found a charity, start a school, go on a vision quest or walkabout, or just sit still and meditate.

The time to do what your heart wants is now, because these days mark the beginning of the end of time: as time accelerates toward the speed of light we will finally run out of time. Soon, we will have finally arrived at the finish line of the now.

That day will mark the end of the tyranny of time. No longer will you mark your days with a clock, instead, your day will be as long as you want it to be; instead of marking time, spending time, wasting time, or running out of time, you will be able to make time to be whatever you want to be.

The end of time will come when we finally do whatever makes us most happy, when we are finally here and now. When we follow our hearts, which always tell us true, we become timeless and eternal. And so the paradigm shifts, time ends, and your real life can finally begin.

-:-:-:-:-

A grassroots movement such as social media naturally favors the individual who exhibits community-driven values of integrity, value, service, and vision. Your integrity, your service, and your vision combined with the trust that you inspire in others—that's what builds a healthy community. Establish your brand, nurture your contacts, enhance your reputation, help others, and don't forget to always give value.

Social media communities are self-sustaining. The same community that hires you and buys from you also supplies you with the contacts, goods, employees, and services that you need. Social media continuously generates new opportunities for all.

The viral freeways of social media can facilitate your business and personal life in ways that were completely unforeseen a few years ago. Our tools are indeed changing us. Together, we can step up to the plate and build a better future. Like they say,

If you build it, they will come.

About the Author

Aliyah Marr is the author of several books on creativity and self-actualization. She is a creative director with a client list of Fortune 500 companies and a creative consultant for entrepreneurs. As an educator, she taught graphic design, art, interactive programming, and new media at Parsons, Pratt and The School of Visual Art in New York City.

She founded several groups on Linked In, including Caffeinated Creatives. Along the way, she has acquired too many blogs, websites, and Twitter accounts to manage, so she knows first hand that you should never let social media run your life. Currently the author is working on her next book and is available for seminars, speaking engagements, and private coaching.

Also by Aliyah Marr

The Tarot of Creativity
The Oracle of Creative Transformation

The Tarot Key
Unlock the Secrets of Your Soul

Parallel Mind The Art of Creativity
The (missing) Manual for Your Right Brain

The Creative Life in 365 Degrees
*Daily Inspiration, Wisdom, and
Comfort for the Creative Soul*

Celestial Journey
The Voyage of the Creative Spirit

Squawk!
Social Media for the Solitary Bird

-:-:-:-:-

www.parallelmindzz.com
tools & toys for creative people

Did you like this book?

I would appreciate it if you would
post a review via the page below:

http://amzn.to/2ebkotB

Thank you!

Aliyah Marr